100 years *of* Popu

900   1920   1930   1940   1950   1960   1970   1980   1990   2000

Product Line Manager:
Carol Cuellar

Assistant Product Line Editor:
Donna Salzburg

Book Cover and Design:
JPCreativeGroup.com

CONTENTS

Title	Page

CONTENTS

Title	Page

AIN'T WE GOT FUN

Words and Music by
GUS KAHN, RAYMOND B. EGAN
and RICHARD A. WHITING

Moderato

Ain't We Got Fun - 4 - 1

CHORUS

ALABAMY BOUND

Words by
B.G. DeSYLVA and BUD GREEN

Music by
RAY HENDERSON

AM I BLUE?

Words by
GRANT CLARKE

Music by
HARRY AKST

Am I Blue? - 3 - 1

AMONG MY SOUVENIRS

Words by
EDGAR LESLIE

Music by
HORATIO NICHOLLS

ANY TIME

Words and Music by
HERBERT "HAPPY" LAWSON

Any Time - 2 - 1

APRIL SHOWERS

Words by
B.G. DeSYLVA

Music by
LOUIS SILVERS

AVALON

Words by
AL JOLSON and B.G. DeSYLVA

Music by
VINCENT ROSE

Avalon - 3 - 1

THE BIRTH OF THE BLUES

Words by
B.G. DeSYLVA and LEW BROWN

Music by
RAY HENDERSON

THE BEST THINGS IN LIFE ARE FREE

Words and Music by
B.G. DeSYLVA, LEW BROWN
and RAY HENDERSON

The Best Things in Life Are Free - 2 - 1

BLACK BOTTOM

Words by
B.G. DeSYLVA and LEW BROWN

Music by
RAY HENDERSON

Black Bottom - 2 - 1

BYE BYE BLACKBIRD

Words by
MORT DIXON

Music by
RAY HENDERSON

BUTTON UP YOUR OVERCOAT

Words and Music by
B.G. DeSYLVA, LEW BROWN
and RAY HENDERSON

CALIFORNIA HERE I COME

Words and Music by
AL JOLSON, BUD DeSYLVA
and JOSEPH MEYERS

CHARLESTON

Words and Music by
CECIL MACK and JIMMY JOHNSON

Car-o-lin - a, Car-o-lin - a, At last they're got you on the map,

With a new tune, Fun-ny blue tune,

Charleston - 4 - 1

CLAP HANDS!
Here Comes Charley

Words by
BILLY ROSE and BALLARD MacDONALD

Music by
JOSEPH MEYER

Clap hands! Here comes Char-ley; Clap hands! Good time Char-ley; Clap hands!
Clap hands! Here comes Char-ley; Clap hands! Good time Char-ley; Clap hands!

Here comes Char-ley now. This way — join the part-y;
Here comes Char-ley now. This way — meet the dol-lies,

I say — meet Mc-Carth-y; Hey! Hey! Char-ley, take a bow
I say — Zieg-field Fol-lies; Hey! Hey! Char-ley, take a bow

Clap Hands! - 2 - 1

CLAP YO' HANDS

Music and Lyrics by
GEORGE GERSHWIN and IRA GERSHWIN

FASCINATING RHYTHM

Music and Lyrics by
GEORGE GERSHWIN and IRA GERSHWIN

Fascinating Rhythm - 4 - 1

Won't you take a day off? De - cide to run a-long Some-where far a-way off, And make it snap-py! Oh, how I long to be _ the man I used to be!

Fas-ci-nat-ing Rhy-thm, Oh, won't you stop pick-ing on me!"

me!"

FIVE FOOT TWO, EYES OF BLUE

Lyric by
SAM LEWIS and JOE YOUNG

Music by
RAY HENDERSON

Five Foot Two, Eyes — 2 - 1

FUNNY FACE

Music and Lyrics by
GEORGE GERSHWIN
and IRA GERSHWIN

He: Frank - ie, dear, your birth - day gift re -
She: Need - n't tell me that I'm not so

veals to me _____ that at heart you're real - ly not so
pret - ty, dear, _____ when my look - ing glass and I a -

bad. _____ If I add your fun - ny face ap -
gree. _____ In the con - test at At - lan - tic

Funny Face - 4 - 1

CAN'T HELP LOVIN' DAT MAN

Words by
OSCAR HAMMERSTEIN II

Music by
JEROME KERN

Can't Help Lovin' Dat Man - 3 - 1

GET HAPPY

Words and Music by
HAROLD ARLEN and TED KOEHLER

Get Happy - 3 - 1

HALLELUJAH!

Words by
LEO ROBIN and CLIFFORD GREY

Music by
VINCENT YOUMANS

Hallelujah! - 4 - 1

How I sang a - bout the Judge-ment morn,

And of Ga - briel toot-in' on his horn. In that

sun - ny land of milk and hon - ey, I had no com-plaints,

While I thought of Saints So I say to all who feel for - lorn:

Hallelujah! - 4 - 2

65

HAPPY DAYS ARE HERE AGAIN

Words by
JACK YELLEN

Music by
MILTON AGER

Happy Days Are Here Again - 4 - 1

GIVE MY REGARDS TO BROADWAY

Words and Music by
GEORGE M. COHAN

Tempo di Marcia

At a port in France one morn-ing wait-ing for my
Say hel-lo to dear old Con-ey Isle, if for there you

ship to sail,_____ Yan-kee sol-diers on a fur-lough came to
chance to be,_____ When you're at the Wal-dorf have a smile and

get the lat-est mail;_____ I_____ told them I was oh my
charge it up to me;_____ Men-tion my name ev-'ry place you

Give My Regards to Broadway - 3 - 1

way to old Man - hat - tan Isle;_____ They all gath - ered a -
go, as 'round the town you roam;_____ Wish you'd call on my

bout, As the Ves - sel pulled out and said with a smile._____
gal, Now re - mem - ber, old pal, when you get back home._____

CHORUS

Give my re - gards to Broad - - way, re - mem - ber me to

Her - ald Square,_____ Tell all the gang at For - ty - -

Give My Regards to Broadway - 3 - 2

HARD-HEARTED HANNAH
(The Vamp of Savannah)

Words and Music by
JACK YELLEN, MILTON AGER,
BOB BIGELOW and CHARLES BATES

Moderato

In old Sa-van-nah, I said, Sa-van-nah, The weath-er there is nice and warm;—
You ought to see her, You ought to see her, Out-side she's just as soft as silk;—

The cli-mate's of the south-ern brand,— But here's what I don't un-der-stand;—
But so-cial-ly she's hard as nails,— She's just a gal who hates the males!—

They've got a gal there, A pret-ty gal there, Who's cold-er than an
And when she's nas-ty, Oh, when she's nas-ty, She's 'bout as sweet as

arc-tic storm;_Got a heart just like a stone;___ E - ven ice-men leave her a-lone,___
sour milk;_Noth-ing she likes bet-ter than ___ Feed-in' pois-oned food to a man,___

REFRAIN

They call her HARD HEART- ED HAN-NAH, the vamp of Sa-van-nah,
They call her HARD HEART- ED HAN-NAH, the vamp of Sa-van-nah,

The mean-est gal in town;__ Leath-er is tough but Han-nah's heart is tough-er;
The mean-est gal in town;__ Talk of your cold, re-frig - er - at - ing Mam-mas,

She's a gal_who loves to see men suf-fer! To tease 'em and thrill 'em, To
Broth-er, she's_the Po-lar bear's pa - jam-as! To tease 'em and thrill 'em, To

HONEYSUCKLE ROSE

Words by
ANDY RAZAF

Music by
THOMAS "FATS" WALLER

HOW LONG HAS THIS BEEN GOING ON?

Music and Lyrics by
GEORGE GERSHWIN and IRA GERSHWIN

He: As a tot, when I trot-ted in lit-tle vel-vet pant ies,
She: 'Neath the stars at ba-zaars of-ten I've had to ca-ress men,

I was kissed by my sis-ters, my cous-ins and my aunt-ies.
Five or ten dol-lars then I'd col-lect from all those yes-men.

Sad to tell, it was Hell, an in-fer-no worse than Dan-te's.
Don't be sad, I must add that they meant no more than chess-men.

How Long Has This Been Going On? - 4 - 1

How Long Has This Been Going On? - 4 - 2

82

How Long Has This Been Going On? - 4 - 3

How Long Has This Been Going On? - 4 - 4

THE HAWAIIAN WEDDING SONG
KE KALI NEI AU

English Words by
AL HOFFMAN and DICK MANNING

Hawaiian Words and Music by
CHARLES E. KING

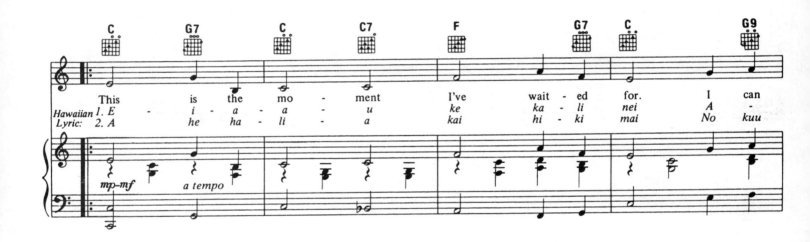

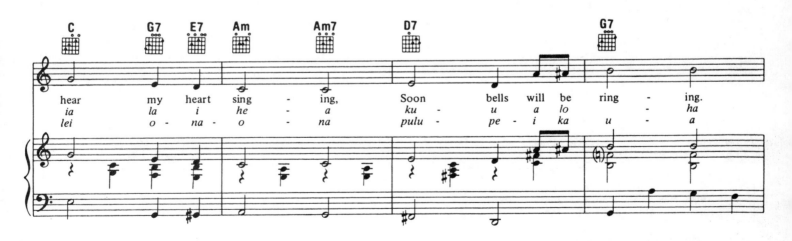

The Hawaiian Wedding Song - 3 - 1

The Hawaiian Wedding Song - 3 - 3

I CAN'T GIVE YOU ANYTHING BUT LOVE

Music by JIMMY McHUGH
Words by DOROTHY FIELDS

I Can't Give You Anything But Love - 3 - 1

I MAY BE WRONG
(But, I Think You're Wonderful!)

Words by
HARRY RUSKIN

Music by
HENRY SULLIVAN

I'M JUST WILD ABOUT HARRY

Words and Music by
NOBLE SISSLE and EUBIE BLAKE

I'm Just Wild About Harry - 3 - 1

I'm Just Wild About Harry - 3 - 3

I WANT TO BE HAPPY

Lyrics by
IRVING CAESAR

Music by
VINCENT YOUMANS

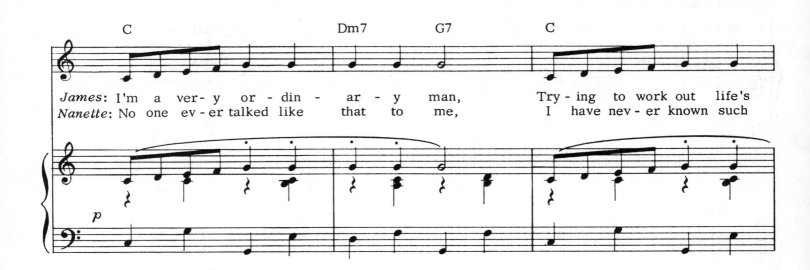

James: I'm a ver-y or-din-ar-y man, Try-ing to work out life's

Nanette: No one ev-er talked like that to me, I have nev-er known such

hap - py plan, Do - ing un - to oth - ers as I'd

sym - pa - thy, On - ly in my dreams, it real - ly

I Want to Be Happy - 4 - 1

I Want to Be Happy - 4 - 2

Refrain

I want to be hap-py, but I won't be hap-py

till I make you hap-py, too; _____

Life's real-ly worth liv-ing, when we are mirth-giv-ing,

Why can't I give some to you? _____ When skies are

I'LL BUILD A STAIRWAY TO PARADISE

Words by
B.G. DeSYLVA and IRA GERSHWIN

Music by
GEORGE GERSHWIN

I'll Build a Stairway to Paradise - 4 - 1

I'M SITTING ON TOP OF THE WORLD

Lyric by
LEWIS and YOUNG

Music by
RAY HENDERSON

I'm sit-ting on top of the world, _____ Just roll-ing a-long, _____ Just roll-ing a-long, _____ I'm quit-ting the blues of the world, _____ Just sing-ing a song, _____ just sing-ing a

I'm Sitting on Top of the World - 2 - 1

IDA, SWEET AS APPLE CIDER

Words by
EDDIE LEONARD

Music by
EDDIE MUNSON

1. In the re - gion where the ros - es al - ways bloom,___
2. When the moon comes steal - ing up be - hind the hill,___

breath - ing out up - on the air their sweet per - fume,___
ev - 'ry-thing a - round me seems so calm and still,___

Ida, Sweet As Apple Cider - 5 - 1

lives a dus-ty maid I long to call my own._____
save the gen-tle call-ing of the Whip - poor Will._____

For I know my love for her will nev - er die._____
Then I long to hold her lit-tle hand in mine._____

When the sun am sin-kin' in dat gold - en West,_____
Thro' the trees the winds are sigh-ing soft and low,_____

Ida, Sweet As Apple Cider - 5 - 2

Lit - tle Rob - in Red Breast gone to seek their nests,_____
seem to come and whis - per that your love is true,_____

Then I sneak down to dat place I love the best._____
Come and be my own now. Sweet - heart do, oh do!_____

Ev - 'ry ev'n - ing there a - lone I sigh._____
Then my life will seem al - most di - vine._____

IF I COULD BE WITH YOU

(One Hour Tonight)

Words and Music by
HENRY CREAMER and
JIMMY JOHNSON

I'm so blue I don't know what to do.
*All dressed up but still no-where to go,

All day through I'm pin-ing just for you. I did wrong when I let you go a-way, for
how I wish that I could see a show. Here I wait with no-one to call me dear. The

* Optional verse.

If I Could Be With You - 3 - 1

INDIAN LOVE CALL

rds by
ARBACH and
OSCAR HAMMERSTEIN II

Music by
RUDOLF FRIML

IT ALL DEPENDS ON YOU

Words and Music by
B.G. DeSYLVA, LEW BROWN
and RAY HENDERSON

Flow-ers de-pend on sun - shine, And the morn-ing dew.
Would-n't it make you proud, dear, If I made a name?

Each thing de-pends on some - thing, And I de-pend on you.
But if I failed to win, dear, Would you want all the blame?

Refrain

I can be hap-py, I can be sad, I can be good or

I can be bad, It all de - pends on you.

IN A LITTLE SPANISH TOWN

('Twas on a Night Like This)

Words by
LEWIS and YOUNG

Music by
MABEL WAYNE

In A Lit-tle Span-ish Town, 'twas on a night like this,

Stars were peek-a-boo-ing down, 'twas on a night like this,

I whis-pered, "Be true to me," _____ And she

In a Little Spanish Town - 2 - 1

IF YOU KNEW SUSIE
(Like I Know Susie)

Words and Music by
B.G. DeSYLVA and JOSEPH MEYER

If You Knew Susie - 3 - 1

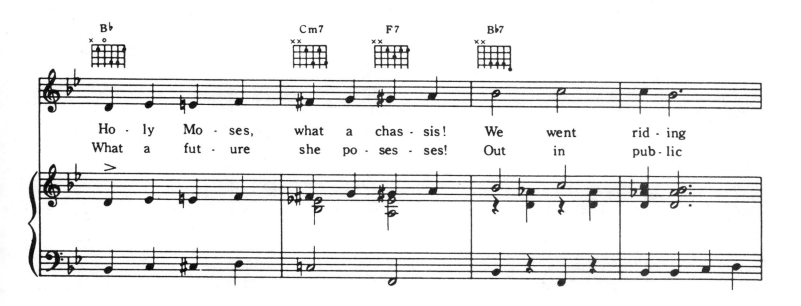

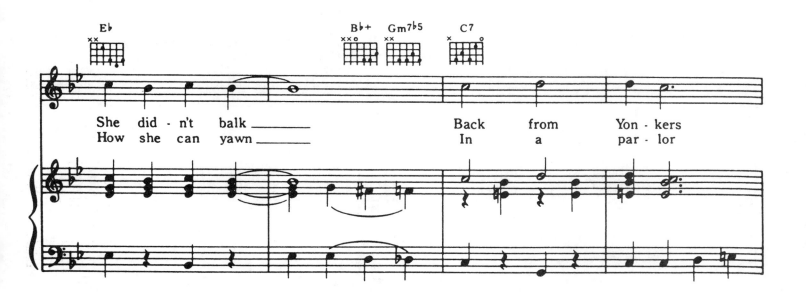

Words by
VERA BLOOM
Spanish Words by
BELEN ORTEGA

JALOUSIE
(Jealousy)

Music by
JACOB GADE

Introduction
Moderato

Jalousie - 5 - 1

130

LET'S DO IT
(Let's Fall in Love)

Words and Music by
COLE PORTER

Let's Do It - 5 - 1

Lith - u - an - i - ans and Letts do it,— Let's do it,—
Ev - en laz - y Jel - ly - fish do it,— Let's do it,—

Let's fall in— love.———— The Dutch in old Am-ster-
Let's fall in— love.———— E-lect-ric eels, I might—

dam do it,— Not to men-tion the Finns Folks in Si-
add, do it,— Though it shocks 'em I know. Why ask if—

LIZA
(All the Clouds'll Roll Away)

Words by
IRA GERSHWIN and GUS KAHN

Music by
GEORGE GERSHWIN

Liza (All the Clouds'll Roll Away) - 3 - 1

LOOK FOR THE SILVER LINING

Words by
B.G. DeSYLVA

Music by
JEROME KERN

Boy: Please don't be of-fend-ed if I
Girl: As I wash my dish-es, I'll be
preach to you a while. Tears are out of place in eyes that were meant to smile.
fol-low-ing your plan, till I see the bright-ness in ev-'ry pot and pan.
There's a way to make your ver-y big-gest trou-bles small.
I am sure your point of view will ease the dai-ly grind.
Here's the hap-py se-cret of it all.
So I'll keep re-peat-ing in my mind.

Refrain (slowly, with warm expression)

Look for the sil-ver lin-ing when-e'er a cloud ap-

LOVER, COME BACK TO ME!

Words by
OSCAR HAMMERSTEIN II

Music by
SIGMUND ROMBERG

Lover, Come Back to Me! - 4 - 2

144

Lover, Come Back to Me! - 4 - 3

MA!

(He's Making Eyes at Me)

Lyric by
SIDNEY CLARE

Music by
CON CONRAD

Ma! - 2 - 1

MAKE BELIEVE

Words by
OSCAR HAMMERSTEIN II

Music by
JEROME KERN

Make Believe - 5 - 1

Cmaj7   C7

And if the things we dream a - bout don't hap - pen __ to be

F   Dm7♭5   C/G   Dm/G

so, _____ that's _ just an un - im - por - tant

G7   C   C#dim7

tech - ni - cal - i - ty. _____ We could

Slower

G7

make be - lieve _____ I love you, _____ on - ly

MY BLUE HEAVEN

Words by
GEORGE WHITING

Music by
WALTER DONALDSON

Moderato

Day is end - ing, Birds are wend - ing Back to the shel - ter
Moon - beams creep - ing, Flow'rs are sleep - ing Un - der a star - lit

of
way,

Each lit - tle nest they love.
Wait - ing an - oth - er day.

Night shades fall - ing,
Time for rest - ing,

My Blue Heaven - 3 - 1

MAKIN' WHOOPEE!

Words by
GUS KAHN

Music by
WALTER DONALDSON

Makin' Whoopee! - 2 - 1

THE MAN I LOVE

Music and Lyrics by
GEORGE GERSHWIN and IRA GERSHWIN

Andantino semplice

When the mel-low moon be-gins to beam, Ev-'ry night I dream a lit-tle dream,

And of course Prince Charm-ing is the theme, The he for me. Al-

The Man I Love - 4 - 1

159

The Man I Love - 4 - 2

MOUNTAIN GREENERY

Words by
LORENZ HART

Music by
RICHARD RODGERS

Moderato

mf

rall.

C   Am   Dm7   G7   C   Am   Dm7   G7

p-f

In   a   moun-tain   green-er-y,   where   God   paints   the   scen-er-y
In   a   moun-tain   green-er-y,   where   God   paints   the   scen-er-y

C   F   D7   G   Am7   G°   2fr.   G

just   two   craz-y   peo-ple   to-geth-er;
just   two   craz-y   peo-ple   to-geth-er;

C   Am   Dm7   G7   C   Am   Dm7   G7

mp

while   you   love   your   lov-er,   let   blue   skies   be   your   cov-er-let,
how   we   love   se-ques-ter-ing   where   no   pests   are   pest-er-ing,

Mountain Greenery - 2 - 1

Mountain Greenery - 2 - 2

MY HEART STOOD STILL

Words by
LORENZ HART

Music by
RICHARD RODGERS

My Heart Stood Still - 4 - 1

OL' MAN RIVER

Words by
OSCAR HAMMERSTEIN II

Music by
JEROME KERN

Ol' Man River - 5 - 1

RHAPSODY IN BLUE

By
GEORGE GERSHWIN
Paraphrased and Arranged by
HENRY LEVINE

Moderately slow, with expression

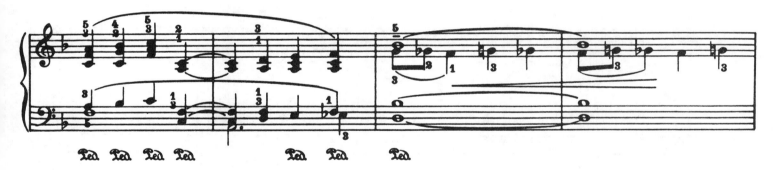

Rhapsody in Blue - 3 - 1

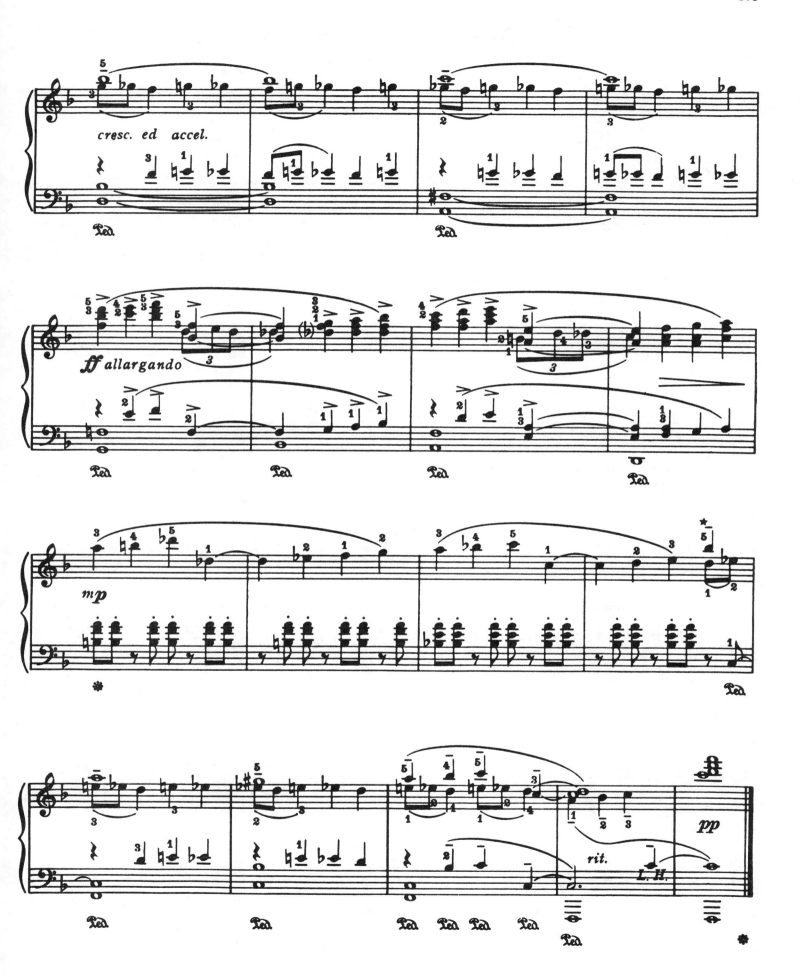

Rhapsody in Blue - 3 - 3

ROCK-A-BYE YOUR BABY
WITH A DIXIE MELODY

Words by
SAM M. LEWIS and JOE YOUNG

Music by
JEAN SCHWARTZ

Rock-A-Bye Your Baby With a Dixie Melody - 4 - 1

ROSE-MARIE

Words by
OTTO HARBACH and
OSCAR HAMMERSTEIN II

Music by
RUDOLF FRIML

Rose-Marie - 4 - 1

Moderato *(molto amabile)*

'S WONDERFUL

Music and Lyrics by
GEORGE GERSHWIN and IRA GERSHWIN

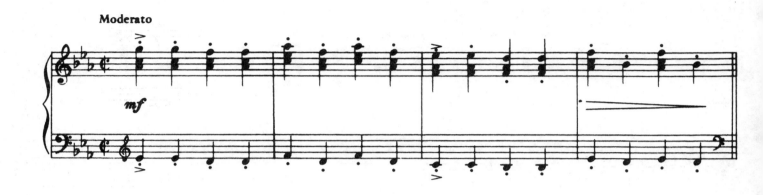

He: Life has just be - gun. Jack has found his Jill,
She: Don't mind tell - ing you, In my hum - ble fash,

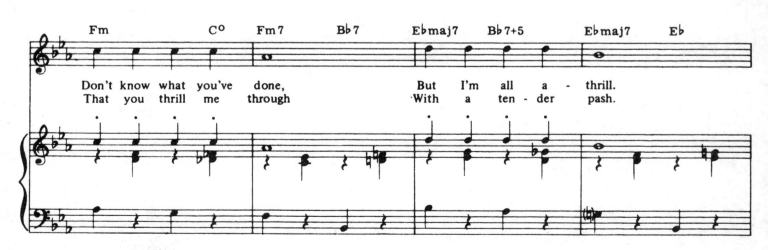

Don't know what you've done, But I'm all a - thrill.
That you thrill me through With a ten - der pash.

'S Wonderful - 4 - 1

SINGIN' IN THE RAIN

Lyric by
ARTHUR FREED

Music by
NACIO HERB BROWN

Singin' in the Rain - 3 - 1

SOME OF THESE DAYS

Words and Music by
SHELTON BROOKS

Some of These Days - 3 - 1

SOMEBODY LOVES ME

Words by
BALLARD MACDONALD and B.G. DeSYLVA
French version by EMELIA RENAUD

Music by
GEORGE GERSHWIN

When this world be-gan
Tout dès le dé - but

It was Heav-en's plan,
Il fut en - ten - du

There should be a girl for ev-'ry sin - gle man;
Qu'il y au - rait pour chaque hom-me u - ne femme;

To my great re - gret
Mais à mon re - gret

Some-one has up - set,
Fut chan - gé l'as - pect

Somebody Loves Me - 4 - 1

Somebody Loves Me - 4 - 4

SOMETIMES I'M HAPPY

Words by
IRVING CAESAR

Music by
VINCENT YOUMANS

Sometimes I'm Happy - 4 - 1

Lyrics:
But when I hate you, it's 'cause I love you.

That's how I am so what can I do?

I'm hap - py when I'm with

you. _____

you. _____

ST. LOUIS BLUES

Words and Music by
W.C. HANDY

St. Louis Blues - 6 - 1

STOUTHEARTED MEN

Words by
OSCAR HAMMERSTEIN II

Music by
SIGMUND ROMBERG

Refrain:

SONNY BOY

Words and Music by
AL JOLSON, B.G. DeSYLVA,
LEW BROWN and RAY HENDERSON

Sonny Boy - 3 - 1

TOOT, TOOT, TOOTSIE!
(Good-bye)

Words and Music by
GUS KAHN, ERNIE ERDMAN,
DAN RUSSO and TED FIORITO

Yes-ter-day I heard a lov-er sigh, ___ "Good - bye ___ oh me, oh
When some-bod-y says good-bye to me, ___ I'm sad ___ as I can

my" ___ Sev - en times he got a-board his train ___ And
be, ___ Not so with this lov-ing Ro - me - o, ___ He

sev - en times he hur-ried back to kiss his love a - gain, and tell her:
seemed to take a lot of pleas-ure say-ing bye-bye to his treas-ure:

Toot, Toot, Tootsie! - 3 - 1

Chorus   Medium Bright

"TOOT, TOOT, TOOT-SIE, Good - Bye! _____ TOOT, TOOT,

TOOT-SIE, don't cry, _____ The choo choo train that takes

me, A - way from you no words can tell how sad it makes me,

Kiss me, Toot-sie, and then, _____ Do it

Toot, Toot, Tootsie! - 3 - 2

THOU SWELL

Words by
LORENZ HART

Music by
RICHARD RODGERS

220

TIP-TOE THRU' THE TULIPS WITH ME

Words by
AL DUBIN

Music by
JOE BURKE

Tip-Toe Thru' the Tulips With Me - 2 - 2

THE VARSITY DRAG

Words and Music by
B.G. DeSYLVA, LEW BROWN
and RAY HENDERSON

The Varsity Drag - 2 - 1

The Varsity Drag - 2 - 2

WAITING FOR THE ROBERT E. LEE

Words and Music by
L. WOLFE GILBERT and LEWIS F. MUIR

WHAT IS THIS THING CALLED LOVE?

Words and Music by
COLE PORTER

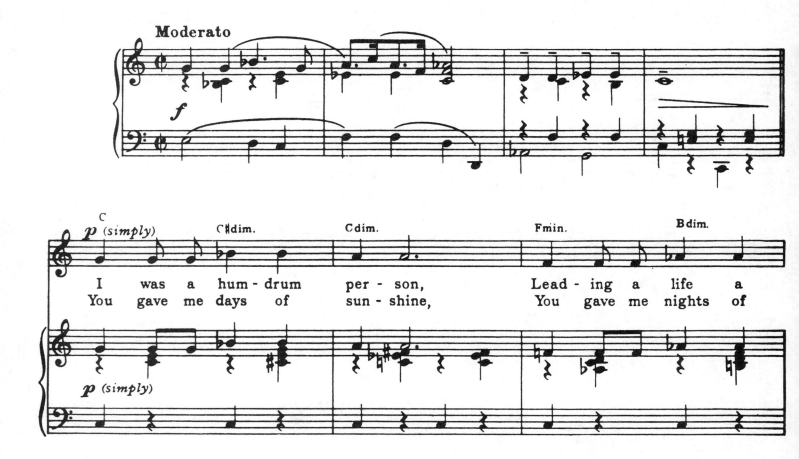

What Is This Thing Called Love? - 4 - 1

WHO?

Lyrics by
OTTO HARBACH and
OSCAR HAMMERSTEIN

Music by
JEROME KERN

Boy who'll know the an-swer when I ask._____
Can be played with la-dies when they say:_____

Who_____ stole my heart____ a-way?

Who_____ makes me dream____ all day? Dreams, I

know, can nev-er be true,____ Seems as

Who? - 3 - 3

WHO'S SORRY NOW?

Words by
BERT KALMAR and HARRY RUBY

Music by
TED SNYDER

236

WHY DO I LOVE YOU?

Words by
OSCAR HAMMERSTEIN II

Music by
JEROME KERN

WITH A SONG IN MY HEART

Words by
LORENZ HART

Music by
RICHARD RODGERS

YOU DO SOMETHING TO ME

Words and Music by
COLE PORTER

You Do Something to Me - 4 - 1

YOU WERE MEANT FOR ME

Words by
ARTHUR FREED

Music by
NACIO HERB BROWN

You Were Meant for Me - 2 - 1

YOU'RE THE CREAM IN MY COFFEE

Words and Music by
B.G. DeSYLVA, LEW BROWN
and RAY HENDERSON

You're the Cream in My Coffee - 4 - 1

You're the Cream in My Coffee - 4 - 4

EVERYBODY LOVES MY BABY

Key of F (D minor)(D-C)

Tune Uke

G C E A

Words and Music by
JACK PALMER and SPENCER WILLIAMS

1. I'm as hap-py as a king,— Feel-in' good 'n' ev-'ry-thing.— I'm just like a bird in Spring, Got to let it out. It's my sweet-ie, can't you guess?— Wild a-bout her, I'll con-fess; Does she love me? Oh, my, yes! That's just why I shout:

2. Ev-'ry-where my ba-by goes,— Dressed up in the swell-est clothes; She just vamps a gang of beaux, But that's all bush-'wa. They all try to set a pace,— Just to see who'll be the ace; Then she puts them in their place, When they go too far.

Everybody Loves My Baby - 3 - 1